Horace P. Biddle

Russian Literature

Horace P. Biddle

Russian Literature

ISBN/EAN: 9783337165048

Printed in Europe, USA, Canada, Australia, Japan

Cover: Foto ©Thomas Meinert / pixelio.de

More available books at **www.hansebooks.com**

RUSSIAN LITERATURE.

BY

HORACE P. BIDDLE.

CINCINNATI:
Robert Clarke & Co., Printers,
1877.

RUSSIAN LITERATURE.

SINCE the Crimean war, in 1855, the power of Russia, although it suffered in that contest, has been much more noticed by other nations than it had been before; and since the abolition of serfdom in her dominion, in 1861, her government has become a study for other statesmen besides her own : but no nation yet has given her literature more than a passing notice. The reason may be plain. Her great military power is felt by the world, and her policy, in reference to the law of nations, has its influence, but her literature, which will ultimately represent the best results of all her powers, is not yet established. Perhaps her banner may yet wave, her policy rule, and her language be heard, from the chilling snows of Siberia to the burning rays of Good Hope—for she is rapidly availing herself of the science, art, and skill of other nations—if so, then her literature will be known to the world ; for the school and college, in the range of time, are more powerful than the cabinet and the field.

Literature is as enduring as human nature, and had its beginning almost coeval with the origin of mankind. The traditions, observations, and tales of love and battle, form the bases of the first rude essays of the historian, the philosopher, and the poet. Poetry precedes civilization—not, indeed, in the shape

of regular poems, but in bold expression and striking
metaphor; tradition is ever the precursor of authentic history, and observation is the only true basis of
philosophy.   The arts began early in the history of
man.   Necessity invents the useful arts, and the love
of the beautiful, implanted in our nature, suggests
the fine arts.   After myths have passed away like the
clouds of the sky, or the fogs of the sea; after traditions have been winnowed of their fictions, and
furnished their grains of truth; after philosophy has
studied the universe and its laws, then comes science,
which is what we know; and all of these together
constitute a nation's literature.   Whenever a nation
begins, it begins a history, a philosophy, the arts
and sciences, and a literature.   But amongst a people, where man has to struggle with the elements and
his enemies for mere animal existence, although he
necessarily acquires knowledge, there are but few joys
for the mind and heart; yet in more polished nations
literature gradually becomes a want of the soul, almost as much as bread is a want of the body.   Literature, indeed, may be defined to be the recorded
culture of the mind and the soul; and the best literature is the best thoughts, upon the best subjects,
expressed in the best words.   The orator and the
poet precede the scholar and the author.   The scholar
learns from the poet, the author reads, invents, and
imagines; the critic comes last.   He draws his rules
from those who spoke, wrote, and sung, without
rules, save the great rule of nature; and the bold
oratory and artless song of the savage sometimes
have a beauty which no learning or criticism can im-
prove.   Kings, princes, heroes, warriors, statesmen,

and rulers, however useful to their times, however wise, brilliant, or accomplished, pass away with their periods; while the man of letters represents pure thought, which remains like the fixed stars ; and he is often remembered for a single sentence, a line, a verse, a principle, a sentiment, simply expressed in words, long after kings, princes, heroes, warriors, statesmen, and rulers are buried beneath the dust of ages, and forgotten forever.

The earliest authentic history of the Slavonic nations, of which Russia is the great modern exponent, fades away amidst the traditions, legends, and tales which have just been noticed. Herodotus mentions a people which are supposed to have been a tribe of the Slavi ; and some allusions to their country and race are made by Strabo, Pliny, and Tacitus. From the resemblance of the Slavonic language to the Sanscrit it has been supposed that these people came from India, but when they passed over into the regions they now occupy, can not be ascertained; probably it was before the Christian era, but the first authentic intelligence with regard to them does not reach back farther than the sixth century. Doubtless the whole Slavonic race originally spoke the same language, but it was soon broken up into dialects, as a language spread over a vast region of country will be—especially while it remains unwritten. The Slavonic language has become varied and enriched by the Greek, Latin, German, French, and even English, and has now ripened into the modern Russian ; but the earliest manuscripts in the Slavonic language are not older than the time of the eleventh century. There are some inscriptions and devices upon the crosses and monuments perhaps older than that date. The earliest records by native writers were written about the middle of the eleventh century. A code of laws was enacted as early as 1280, and recorded in the native language. And Russia, like Greece, and indeed like most other nations, has its epic poem. It is called "Igor's Expedition," and is supposed to have been written in the twelfth century. It is said to possess a refinement and delicacy remarkable for so rude a people as they were at that time, and also has much power and gracefulness; but the critics do not place it very high as a literary production. In the fifteenth century Russian literature received an important influence from the liberality of some of the native princes, who invited the learned from Germany, Italy, and France into their dominions. About the same time public schools were founded; and the Russian youth were sometimes sent to foreign universities to be educated. The language and literature of Poland, also, about this period commenced having an important effect upon the minds of the Russian people; and subsequently Russia obtained the greater part of her public libraries from the spoliation of Poland, and very much enriched her literature from the language and works of that intelligent and brave, but unfortunate people. History began to be regularly recorded, and thus assume an authentic and permanent shape; but Russian literature can not be said to have had a beginning before the reign of Peter the Great, at the close of the seventeenth century. He adopted the Russian language in his courts of justice, and in diplomacy, and made it the polite language of the nation. He had type cast, and established presses, and caused many books to be translated into the Russian from other languages—particularly from the German and French; indeed, Peter the Great was to Russia very much what Alfred the Great was to England; still, up to this time even, the Russian language had no systematic grammar, and of course but little attention had been paid to style. But if Peter the Great laid the foundation of Russian literature, Lomonosof must be regarded as its architect. As most great benefactors are, he was humbly born; his father was a fisherman. He first learned to read from the servants of the church, and so ardent was his desire for knowledge, that he left the shelter of his father's roof clandestinely, and went to Moscow, where, he had been told, they taught the languages; thence to St. Petersburg, where he obtained a liberal education. Afterwards he traveled through Germany and Holland, where he studied philosophy and the sciences. His Russian grammar brought his native language from chaos into order, and he was the first one who cultivated style. He sketched the history of his country, and wrote several works on chemistry and mineralogy. He also composed a long epic poem, as well as several odes and tragedies, but they do not rank high; he was rather a philosopher than a poet. His works are blemished, however, by the too common fault of all who write under tyranny, namely, an undue tendency to panegyric, and a stooping to despotic power. These are weaknesses in a great mind, but the age and country in which he lived must be the excuse of Lomonosof. Contemporaneous with Lomonosof were Kheraskof and Sumarakof, who were very prolific writers, but not of remarkable genius; although Kheraskof, having written an immense and cumbrous epic poem, was called the Russian Homer. About the same time also lived and flourished Dershavin, a poet of true genius. Although his works were bedazzled with the glory of Catharine, yet the true metal could be discovered beneath the tinsel. He wrote an "Ode to God" of uncommon beauty; it was translated into most of the European languages, and attained the distinguished honor of being printed in letters of gold and hung in the palace of the Chinese Emperor and the Temple of Jeddo. But devotion to power, from which not even Dershavin was exempt, is the weakness of all the literati of Russia. Patriotism is a becoming sentiment, but a literature expressive of that which is not just to all men, can have no abiding place in the Republic of Letters. Catharine was a great patron of learning, but a literature indebted to any other influence than that of truth and nature, can never be pure or permanent.

During the reign of Alexander, who succeeded Catharine, many new schools and several universities were founded, also a number of museums. This prince affected to be a great patron of letters, but his influence rather made learning fashionable than afforded it any substantial advantage. Writers became extremely numerous; authorship seemed to be a rage with the nobility. Russia, at this time, possessed about fourteen thousand volumes in the Slavonic language, more than seven thousand of which were said to be the product of a single year. We shall be able to mention but few authors of this period — they are very numerous — among whom

Karamzin must stand at the head, for, unquestionably, next to Lomonosof, he was the great benefactor of Russian literature. After fighting awhile in the army with credit, he turned his attention to letters, and established the *Moscow Journal*, a periodical through which he first became known to the world in his new character. He won nobler laurels with his pen than he had done with his sword. At length he enlarged his field by founding another periodical called the *European Messenger*, in which he took a larger and higher range of subjects; but his more permanent fame rests on his history of the Russian Empire. This great work, however, having been written under the patronage of the government, is not free from the blemishes we have before mentioned. If not false in fact, yet the romantic coloring is too apt to gild the deed which truth and justice must condemn. The great advantage which Russian literature gained from Karamzin, was the improvement of its language and the cultivation of a vigorous and idiomatic style.

A remarkable poet of this period, both for genius and misfortune, was Ivan Koslof. Early in life he had been a gay and fashionable man, and pursued his career of dissipation until sickness deprived him of the use of his limbs, soon after which misfortune he lost his sight. Adversity seemed to touch and awaken his true genius. He found a balm for his afflictions in literature. Heine, of Germany, affords a similar and more recent example of the soothing effect of culture under misfortune. Being a lover of the intense and passionate, Koslof imitated and translated Byron, and like that great poet, and like

Heine also, "he learned in suffering what he taught in song." Another poet, of a similar name—Ivan Krylof—was celebrated for the composition of many stories and fables, and his sweet appeals to child-like nature. Count Orloff, as well as several of the literati of Paris, did him the honor to translate his works into the French language. He was a pure, harmless, kind-hearted man, and, notwithstanding the ruggedness of the Russian character, became a great favorite of the nation. Whoever, indeed, obtains a hearing from the youth of a nation secures perpetual fame. At this period Russia had produced but little in the drama; nothing, indeed, in the department of tragedy of any greatness or power. Ozerof is the leading dramatic poet, and his most popular, and perhaps his best play, is entitled the " Miseries of Intellect"—surely a most admirable theme. The novel has been cultivated in Russia, both in prose and rhyme, to a considerable extent. The one best known among the older ones, as far as I am informed, is entitled " *Bursak*," and is said to abound in that pleasing, quiet humor, so characteristic of Don Quixote, but it narrates the adventures of a scholar with his pen, instead of a knight-errant with his sword. Recently Russia has produced a novelist of great power—Ivan S. Turgenef—still living. His first venture—"Notes of a Sportsman "—a series of sketches of country life, contains vigorous attacks upon the villeinage of the serfs, and had much to do, it is thought, in abolishing that odious system of slavery. These sketches were followed by more elaborate works—" Fathers and Children," "Smoke," "A Nest of Nobles," " The

Unfortunate One," etc.—all upon Russian subjects, and written with great vigor.

Translations have even abounded in Russia. Homer, Ossian, Ariosto, Tasso, Pope, Byron, in poetry; Newton, Locke, and Bacon, in philosophy; and a great number of ecclesiastical and educational works have received the Slavonic dress.

The reign of the late Emperor Nicholas commenced in a storm—indeed in blood, and ended in storm and blood. The most of his rule, however, was calm, but it was the calm of force, not of consent. Many of the young literati were concerned in the bloody tragedy which ushered the emperor into power, and lost their lives in the contest. His death, during the terrible war in the Crimea, will be long remembered. The conflict was really between free thought and despotic power. The Russian Pegasus had become restive under the curb and rein of tyranny. He longed to range at liberty in fresh pastures, and drink from a pure Hippocrene, or dash his daring hoof on Parnassus Mount; but, alas! he was subjugated to the Emperor's will, and compelled to drudge in his iron service, just as Napoleon III geared him to the car of tyranny in France.

Research and criticism began to assume a more prominent part in literature during the late reign than it had previously done. A periodical work, entitled "The Telegraph," was established by Polevoi, who was a self-made man—not having been bred to letters, nor was he a man of much genius—but he possessed a clear judgment and great energy of thought, the very qualities which constitute the critic. History and biography assumed more im-

portance, but no work of philosophy or science, or
at least none of a high order, had yet appeared written by a Russian, or in the Slavonic language. Religious controversies arose, and skepticism and infi-
delity made their appearance during this reign,
probably transplanted from Germany and France.
Panslavism—a political doctrine, according to which
Russia, being at the head, claimed the right to ab-
sorb all the Slavonic nations into her own empire—
was much discussed at this period, and was indeed
the principle which gave the final blow to the liberty
of Poland.   Books of travel and studies of antiqui-
ties now appeared, but they formed no very considerable branch of Russian literature.   Novels were
very numerous and began to portray Russian home-
life, but no remarkable author appeared in this line.
Their works were all ephemeral, corresponding to
the multitude of tales which we now find in our own
nation.   Pushkin, the greatest poet that Russia has
yet produced, flourished during this time.   He had
been banished by Alexander for his too daring sentiments of liberty, but on account of his great genius
was recalled by Nicholas.   During his exile he wrote
much and well, but on his return he seemed to have
lost the spirit of his genius, so baleful is the influence of a despotic court upon this noble principle.
His writings possess the true Byronic fire, and,
like those of Koslof, evidently share the influence of
the great English bard. Pushkin, indeed, may be
called the Russian Byron.   He had the daring of an
eagle, and behind the bars of despotism, like the
caged eagle, could only gaze upon the sky of liberty.
The court of Nicholas was also adorned by a num-

ber of minor poets, amongst whom two ladies of some
genius appeared, the Princess Volkanski, and Miss
Teplef. Mrs. Helena Han was also an author of
celebrity, whose writings resemble those of the late
Madame George Sand. A collection of the popular
poetry of the Slavonic tribes has been made by Bie-
lowski, a Polander, by which it appears that Russia,
though the largest, is not the oldest nor the most
poetical branch of this extensive family. But Russian poetry, comparing it in quality to that of this
prolific age in our own country, is very limited in
its production. The Russians can not be said to be
a poetical people. Pushkin is their only great poet
when compared with the poets of other nations.
The drama, during the reign of Nicholas, lay at the
feet of the Emperor. The very titles of the plays
are abject, and sometimes even sacrilegious; for in-
stance, one is called, "Our Lives Belong to the
Czar," another, "The Hand of God Defends the
Czar."

Polish literature, although now embraced in the
general name of Russian, of which, however, it is
the greater and better part, still deserves a separate
notice. The language of Poland, like that of Russia,
arose out of the Slavonic dialects, but has been modi-
fied, of course, by the surrounding languages. No
living language can remain permanent ; even the
written language of the Chinese, the most peculiar
of all languages, is now changing under the pressure
of surrounding influences. Like the Egyptian hier-
oglyphics, the key to its meaning has been discovered,
and it no longer remains a mystery. The Polish
tongue is still spoken by ten millions of people.

The earliest production in this language is a war
song—which is still sung, or at least was before the
Partition of Poland amongst the conquering powers
—supposed to have been written about the close of the
tenth century. It should be remembered that Poland
had no existence as a nation, separate from the Slavonic tribes, earlier than the tenth century, nor, indeed,
had Russia earlier than the ninth. This song, which
rather resembles a prayer, has no poetical value, and
notwithstanding so early a specimen, the beginning
of Polish literature does not date before the fifteenth
century.   There are a few slight traces of recorded
thought throughout this dreary period, but nothing
that remains permanent.   Indeed, all the nations of
the earth, except some in the East, during these five
centuries, and the five immediately preceding them,
were robbed of their rights, ensnared in ecclesiastical
meshes, enchained by political tyranny, and trodden
down to the deepest degradation.   The sun of literature, during one thousand years, was obscured by the
clouds of superstition ; philosophy was denied,
science condemned, the arts—except where they sub-
served the interests of the church—were ignored, and
liberty destroyed.   From the tenth to the fifteenth
century, Polish thought and Polish letters were wholly
governed by church dignitaries, who were all foreign-
ers, the nation not being allowed to exercise even
the humblest clerical privileges.   While a nation is
thus robbed and ridden, it is very easy to see why it
produces no literature.   The mind must be free, or
its thoughts are worthless.

Casimir was the first wise Polish prince; he im-
proved the laws, established courts of justice, and

laid the foundation of a national education. He was the Peter the Great of Poland. The first printing press was erected at Cracow, in .1488, from which period the Polish language may be said to date. There has been found, however, a work called " The Memoirs of a Janissary," written at an earlier period, but its language is so imperfect that a modern Pole can not read it without explanation. It is the journal of a Polish nobleman, who joined the Turkish army, and fought at the siege of Constantinople, in 1453; and of course, the true date of the work could not have been long after that event. Some religious works, that bear date about the same time, are still extant, but their language is also so imperfect that they afford conclusive proof of the true commencement of Polish letters. The annals of Poland, however, seem to be correctly written at this time, and for a long period before, but they are found in the Latin language, and written by foreign scholars.

Kochanowski was the founder of Polish literature. He was a man of genius, a scholar, and a poet. His translations of Homer, Anacreon, and Horace, are distinguished for force of language and purity of style; and his original pieces possess uncommon vigor and beauty. He was a dramatic as well as a lyrical poet. Rybinski and Klonowitz were also distinguished as poets; the former wrote in the Latin as well as in the Polish language, and was created a poet-laureate. Karpinski was the poet of the people, and may justly be called the Burns of Poland. From this period, Poland has had a continued succession of poets—too numerous to name even—of a high order in all the departments of the art, down to the time she lost her nationality ; and there is one noble trait of character, which, during all of this time, must forever distinguish them from the Russian poets of the same period—their muse was devoted to freedom ; but, alas, for the sad effect of despotic power in chaining genius—a recent volume of poetry, published at Warsaw, celebrates the praises of all the tyrants of Russia, from Rurik to Alexander. And eloquence, before the downfall of Poland, was also highly cultivated, and very much esteemed, as it always is in a free nation, and as it never can be under a despotism. Russia has never produced a single orator of eminence, whilst Poland has had her hundreds; but, alas, for Polish eloquence, that, too, has been hushed forever.

The novel has been cultivated, perhaps, in Poland, less than any other department of literature, yet Scott has been happily imitated. Sharbeck is the principal, or, at least, one of the leading Polish novelists ; but the novel which is said to be most read, was written by a woman, the Princess of Wirtemberg, and is called, "The Intimations of the Heart"—a very pleasing title, and a subject which a woman could most happily treat. Historians and annalists have abounded in Poland—none of the highest order, however ; but the true history of Poland can never be written. Her nationality is lost, her libraries are plundered, and her archives destroyed. Russia seems determined, under the fatal doctrine of Panslavism, not only to destroy her from amongst the nations of the earth, but also to efface every mark that might seem to indicate her former existence. She was too learned, too eloquent, too brave, and too free, to suit

the designs of Russia; and the remains of her noble
qualities but ill comport with despotic power.

In philosophy, mathematics, astronomy, and the
practical sciences, Poland, for three hundred years
before her downfall, stood equal to any of the contemporaneous nations; while Russia, proper, in
these departments, fell below mediocrity. The universities, seats of learning, down to the common
schools of Poland, were broken up, their funds taken
from them, and every vestige worth removing, trans-
ferred to the halls of the Czar. Since the downfall
of Poland, the more spirited of her people have been
wanderers, too proud to wear the chains of slavery on
their native soil. A great many of her literati fled
to Paris, where they or their descendants still live.
From that city, during the last forty years, they have
published to the world many interesting productions
concerning Poland. " Evening Hours of a Pilgrim,"
the very title of which touches the heart, is a work
of peculiar interest. It gives much information concerning the former condition of Poland, especially
in the time of Poniatowski. I do not know the author of this work; it was published without his
name. The lectures of Mickiéwiczs on Slavonic
literature, delivered at Paris, in the French language,
and afterward published in German, at Leipsic, are
full of thought, and glow with enthusiasm. Their
author was a bold orator and a true poet. He fondly
believed in the revolution of the world, which would
restore his wronged country to her legitimate rights,
and unite all the Slavonic nations under a free government. He made use of this beautiful metaphor;
" There will yet be a torch that shall illumine the

world, of which I am but a spark now falling to the ground." But it is in purely poetical creation that Mickiewiczs shrouds his full power. His "Sir Thadeus" is a work of great beauty; and he is also the author of some smaller poems of a very high order. But in poetry he is not a prolific writer; indeed, it might almost be stated as a rule, that the best poets produce the least poetry; at least, good poetry, compared with such as is "hated by gods and men," bears but a small proportion to it. Pebbles are plenty, diamonds are rare. Count Krazinski, however, is considered by many their greatest poet. He has the ethereal mystical power of Shelley, combined with the passionate fire of Byron; indeed, by some he is considered not inferior to these master spirits. There are a number of other poets still living, too many, indeed, to notice separately, some of whom have a highly-cultivated genius. Their songs are wild and daring, or sweet and subdued, as alternately they sing of their once happy, but now unfortunate country. But the echo of their strains will soon die away, and Polish poetry cease to have a living voice.

Finland, as being a considerable portion of the Russian Empire, may claim our attention a moment. The Finns are not of Slavonic blood; they are supposed, by many, to be the same as the *Phinni* mentioned by Ptolemy, or the *Fenni* noticed by Tacitus. They are a brave and hospitable people, but grave and unsocial. Their popular education is in a low state, yet almost every one studies music and poetry. Their poets wear the mythic robes of Ossian, and their music resembles the ancient Gaelic, or that of the early Welsh; but they can scarcely be said to have a recorded literature. Their greatest poem, or collection of poems—it is difficult to say which—is an epic, entitled *Kallawalla.* It has been translated into English, French, and German, and I believe into the Swedish language. It is from this poem, as some have thought, that Longfellow caught the idea of his *Hiawatha.* Kallawalla sings the legends of the Finnish race, and Hiawatha the traditions of the North American Indians. That the legends and traditions of a rude people, though inhabiting different countries, when their circumstances are alike, might resemble, is highly probable; yet there are but few coincidences between the Finns and our Indians. From the strong resemblance between the two poems, not only in form and spirit, but in many of the incidents, and the frequent similarity of thought and sentiment, it seems highly probable that Professor Longfellow took a lively hint from the Finnish epic. Though Longfellow worthily wears the poetic wreath, yet he is too much of a scholar and too devoted to books to be a thoroughly original poet. Not that a man can be too learned to be a poet, yet his genius must bear a due proportion to his learning, else he will take thought at second hand and unconsciously become a copyist. This is precisely the case with the author of Hiawatha; his genius is covered up in his learning; he has not sufficient force to assimilate it, and thus make it his own, or to shake its influence from his mind. The author of Kallawalla is unknown. It has been sung during many generations at the fireside of the Finn, and chanted in the field to lighten his labor. Indeed it has floated in tradition for ages, until it was gathered up by European scholars, or some modern Pisistratus perhaps, and put in its present shape. This renders its authenticity certain, but leaves the name of its author a mystery forever.

We will now notice some of the characteristics of Slavonic popular poetry, and also give a few specimens. The monuments of a nation's muse generally exist in their epics, dramas, histories; these are read by students, scholars, and critics; but the living and flowing poetry of a nation is found in its songs and ballads; these are read, repeated, recited, and sung by the people. The Slavi are a singing race. The faculty called a musical ear is almost universal with them, and their cultivation of a musical taste is remarkable; and, when not at war, singing and playing on an instrument of the lyre kind, similar to a Spanish guitar—in Latin called a *cithara*, in old English a *cittera*, and in Spanish *guitarra*, whence comes the modern name, *guitar*—constitutes quite an occupation, and consumes much of their time. In their poetry they make frequent use of epithets, and the application of some of them, though somewhat monotonous, is indeed beautiful. To give an example—the word *white* is not only applicable to *things*, but to *actions* also. Not only is it used to express the *color*, but also every quality that is pure, or beautiful, or good. They would say of a noble action, "it is a *white* deed;" or if they speak of the Czar, they call him the *white* Czar; and indeed they extend the application of the epithet to the Almighty, calling Him the *white* God, as we would say the Immaculate. Slavonic poetry is extremely ancient.

We are indebted to German scholars for bringing it
to light, as we are indebted to them for light upon
many other subjects. Its morality, for a rude people, is extremely high and just, and its tone remarkably pure and chaste, as is more likely to be the case
in northern than in southern races. In these respects
politer nations might have learned justice and purity
from the ancient Slavi. It is also comparatively free
from superstition and those monstrous conceptions
which are so apt to disfigure the poetry of rude
nations. Such supernatural expressions as we find in
it generally relate to the attributes of the Supreme
Being, or to the missions of angels, which are pleasing to the most enlightened minds. The belief,
however, in the foreboding of dreams prevails to
some extent. Indeed, but few persons rise entirely
above such influences ; the reason condemns them,
but a doubt will still linger in the sentiments. There
is a prevailing cast of melancholy in the Russian
songs, and in the tone of their national music. The
origin of their popular tunes is as deeply hidden in
the past as the sources of their poetry. They are
rich and varied, and are much admired by cultivated
musicians. The pensiveness which pervades his
songs appears in singular contrast with the generally
cheerful disposition and rugged character of the
hardy Russ. And as warlike as the Russians are,
we yet find but few war songs in their poetry ; nor
are they remarkable for their fire or force when they
do occur. The following "Song of the Haidamack" is a fair specimen. It is expressive of the
Russian's hatred of the Pole. Haidamack is a name
given to the Russian peasant :

SONG OF THE HAIDAMACK.

Gladly would I to the war—
    To the war so full of prey;
Pleasure of the Haidamack,
    But the steward bids me stay!

Gladly to the merry dance,
    Would I to the gusli play,
Pleasure of the rosy maid;
    But the steward bids me stay!

Gladly would I hunting go
    With my hounding dog away,
Pleasure of the noble youth,
    But the steward bids me stay!

But farewell, thou rosy maid,
    Quickly, sabre, to thy goal,
Mount thy charger, Haidamack,
    Perish may the haughty Pole!

Neither are elegiac pieces common in Slavonic poetry. The following elegy, however, on a murdered youth, is supposed to date as early as the sixteenth century:

ELEGY ON A MURDERED YOUTH.

Oh, thou field, thou green and level field,
Oh, thou plain, so far and wide around,
Pleasing field, dressed up with everything—
Everything—with sky-blue flowers so small;
Fresh thy verdure, and thy bushes fledged,
But defaced by one thing—only one!

In thy very middle stands a tree;
On that tree a young grey eagle sits;
He sucks the raven's heart-blood glowing hot,

Drenches with it, too, the moistened earth.
Ah, black raven, youth so good and brave,
Thy destroyer is the eagle grey !

Not a swallow can more fondly cling—
Hovering cling, unto her soft, warm nest,
Than the mother to her murdered son.
And her tears flow like the rushing stream,
And his sister's like the murmuring rill ;
Thus, in showers, the tears of love fall down !

The following touching little piece, entitled " The Dove," may also rank under the present division :

THE DOVE.

On an oak tree sat,
Sat a pair of doves ;
And they heart to heart
Tenderly embraced.

On them suddenly
Darted down a hawk ;
One he seized and tore,
Tore the little dove ;
With his feathered feet,
Soft blue little dove ;
And he poured his blood
Streaming down the tree ;
Feathers too he strewed
Wide around the lea ;
High away the down
Floated on the air.

Ah, how wept and wept,
Ah, how sobbed and sobbed,
The tender doveling then
For her little dove !

Spake the light young hawk
To the little dove ;
" Weep not, weep not so,
Tender little bird !
O'er the sea away—
O'er the far blue sea,
Flocks of other doves
I will drive to thee ;
From them choose thee one,
Choose one soft and blue,
With his feathered feet,
Little dove for you ! "

Said the doveling then,
To the light young hawk :
" Villain, fly thou not
O'er the far blue sea,
Flocks of other doves
Drive not here to me ;
Of all the flocks of doves,
Of all beyond the sea,
The father of my little ones
Alone can comfort me ! "

The song of the Post Boy is highly characteristic
of the rugged Russian and the cheerless climate.
Imagine him in the depths of a Russian winter,
scaling the snow-clad mountain ; in the wild forest ;
through the keen air ; while a few stray sunbeams
glitter on the snow they can not melt, chanting the
following strain :

SONG OF THE POST BOY.

Ah, thou bright sunlight—
Bright and red sunlight,
O'er the mountain high,
Shining through the oak,

Warm the post-boy's heart,
Warm, oh, warm me, sun,
And not me alone,
But my maiden, too !

Ah ! thou maiden dear,
Fairest, dearest child ;
Thou my lovely maid,
Mild and sweet to me !

Black those brows of thine,
Black thy winning eyes,
And thy lovely face,
All so round and bright,
Without painting red,
Without painting white !

To thy girdle rolls
Many a flowing lock ;
And thy voice is sweet,
Full of gentle talk !

In the collections of Slavonic poetry to which I have had access I do not find a single drinking song.

Some of them, however, allude to the vine in rather merry terms. The Russians are known to be a sober, hardy people ; yet, as every poetic literature of which I have any knowledge, has something inspired by the wine-cup, it would seem highly probable that the Russian did not stand as an exception so remarkable. Bacchanalian songs really disfigure Greek and Roman poetry ; and the German, French, and English are not without serious faults in this respect. It is a subject well enough when delicately managed, but in the poet's hands very liable to be abused.

The love of the dead appears to be a strong trait
in the Slavonic character.   The following piece, although it sounds very Germanlike, is characteristic
of the melancholy Slavi.   It is difficult, in these
specimens, to always employ rhyme and exactly pre-
serve the sense, yet it will be attempted in some of
the following pieces :

THE DEAD LOVE.

I sought the dark wood where the oat-grass was growing ;
The maidens were there and the oat-grass were mowing ;
And I called to those maidens : "Now, say, if there be
The maiden I love 'midst the maidens I see !"

And they sighed as they answered : "No, no ; alas, no ;
She was laid in the tomb just one week ago."
" Then show me the way my footsteps must tread
To reach the dark chamber where slumbers the dead !"

" The path is before thee, her grave will be known
By the rosemary wreathes her companions have thrown."
" And where is the church-yard, whose newly-made heaps
Will point out the bed where the blessed one sleeps !"

I turned, and with heart-chilling terror I froze,
As a newly-made grave in my pathway arose ;
And I heard a low voice, but it audibly said :
" Disturb not, disturb not, the peace of the dead !"

" Who treads on my grave ? what footsteps have swept
The dew from the bed where the weary one slept?"
"Oh maiden, my maiden, speak not thus to me,
My presents were once not unwelcome to thee !"

" Thy presents were welcome, but none could I save,
Not one could I bring with me into the grave ;
Go, then, to my mother, and bid her restore
To thy hands every gift which I valued before !"

" Then cast the gold ring in the depths of the sea,
That eternity's peace may be given to me ;
And sink the white 'kerchief deep, deep in the wave,
That my head may repose undisturbed in the grave ! "

The next is a little piece bearing the same title, which, I think, must be regarded as beautiful. The reader should remember what was said about the word *white*—that it meant not only the color, but also everything that is good, pure, or beautiful :

THE DEAD LOVE.

White art thou my maiden,
 Naught so white as thee ;
Warm my love is, maiden,
 Can not warmer be !

But when dead, my maiden,
 Whiter than before ;
Maiden, now I love thee
 Warmer than before !

The accumulated superlatives in this piece are faults in a strictly critical view. Of course nothing can be whiter than the whitest, nor warmer than the warmest. But the same extravagances have been alleged against Sappho and Shakespeare, and indeed can be pointed out in most of our standard poets. The head may detect such errors but the heart forgives them.

Love is the great element in Slavonic poetry, as it is, indeed, in the poetry of all the nations of the earth. Love—nothing so laughed at, yet nothing so wept over; nothing so ridiculed, yet nothing so obeyed ; nothing so gentle, yet nothing so terrible ;

why wonder, then, since it can move every other passion, that love is the master key to poetry. Strong men and proud women may say what they will—he conquers them, and they obey him. The Russian, with all his ruggedness, is delicate in love. In literature their love songs are less offensive with grossness of passion than perhaps those of almost any other nation. Greece, the politest of ancient nations, and France of modern, fall far below Russia in this respect. There is less ideality in the Russian's love than in the Grecian or German, but his affection is more self-sacrificing to the object beloved. The following verse expresses a pure and noble sentiment. It should be mentioned first, however, that the Asiatic custom, by which the parents dispose absolutely of their children in marriage, prevails throughout the Slavonic nations. A Russian daughter, wherever her love might be placed, would not presume to marry against her parents' discretion. This verse expresses the lover's advice to his beloved after she is betrothed to another, in accordance with parental authority:

> Weep not, weep not, oh, sweet maid ;
> Choose, oh, choose another love.
> Is he better? Thou l't forget me ;
> Is he worse? Then think of me—
> Think of me, sweet one, and weep !

The following, which describes a parting under similar circumstances, it appears to me, must be regarded as a beautiful poem. It is impossible to adopt rhyme, in this piece, without too great a sacrifice of the thought.

THE FAREWELL.

Brightly shining sank the waning moon,
And the sun all beautiful arose,
Not a falcon floated through the air—
Strayed a youth along the river's brim ;
Slowly strayed he on, and dreamingly,
Sighing, walked he to the garden green,
Heart all filled with sorrow, thus he mused :
"All the little birds are now awake,
Greeting, all have sung their morning songs.
But, alas ! that sweetest doveling, mine,
She was my youth's first dawning love,
In her chamber slumbers fast and deep.
Ah, not even her friend is in her dreams,
Ah, no thought of me bedims her soul,
While my heart is torn with wildest grief
That she comes to meet me here no more !"

Stepped the maiden from the chamber then,
Wet, oh, wet with tears her lovely face ;
All with sadness dimmed her eyes so clear,
Feebly drooping hung her snowy arms.
'T was no arrow that had pierced her heart,
'T was no adder that had stung her breast ;
Weeping, thus the lovely maid began :
" Fare thee well, belovèd, fare thee well,
Dearest soul, thy father's noblest son ;
I have been betrothed since yesterday,
Come, to-morrow, troops of wedding guests ;
To the altar I am forced to go ;
I shall be another's then, yet thine,
Forever thine, thine only until death !

Having thus shown the complaint of a despairing
lover for the loss of his mistress, we will present the
following little piece, which expresses the grief of the
maiden for the loss of her lover. The sentiment is
lighter than that of the preceding pieces. Perchance

some inveterate bachelor—unwillingly so, no doubt—will exclaim: "and well it may be, for the maiden's love is lighter than the man's." But be that as it may, here is the piece:

THE FORSAKEN MAIDEN.

Little star, with gloomy ray,
If thou coulds't but cry,
If thou hads't a heart, my star,
Sparks, I'm sure, would from thee fly,
Just as tears fall from mine eye.

All the night with golden sparks
Thou for me woulds't cry,
Since my love intends to wed,
Only cause another maid
Richer is than I !

Nor can this piece rank very high as a composition. It is too much elaborated. The heart utters its grief in the most simple and direct language. It never runs after comparisons. The tone of the piece sounds far more like the song of a lover in his closet than the deep murmur of an injured maiden's heart.

The following poem is very plaintive, and fondly expresses the uneasy longing of the love-stricken one:

ABSENT LOVE.

Winds are blowing, howling,
·   Trees are bending low ;
Oh, my heart is aching,
    Tears in streamlets flow !

Days I count with sorrow,
    And no ends appears,

But my heart is lightened
When I'm shedding tears!

Tears the heart can lighten,
Happy make it not,
But one blissful moment
Ne'er can be forgot!

On the lea so sandy—
Dry, dew-thirsty lea,
Oh, without my lover
Life is dark to me!

Where, dark-browed, belovèd one,
Where, oh, mays't thou be!
Come, oh, see, and wonder
How I weep for thee!

I would fly to thee, love,
But no wings have I;
Withered, parched, without thee
Every hour I die!

But I find that I am quoting quite too freely
from this branch of my subject; I can not leave it,
however, without showing the humorous side of the
universal passion. The following playful banter is
quite pleasing:

THE LIBERAL OFFER.

Flowing waters meet each other,
And the winds they blow and blow;
Sweetheart, with the bright blue eyes,
Looking from the window now;

Do not stand so at the window,
Rather come before the door;
If thou givest me two kisses,
I will give thee ten—or more!

This piece is from Bohemia, and the succeeding one from the Vendee, neither of which provinces belong to Russia, but both are of Slavonic origin. The following verses will show lovers

HOW TO CHOOSE A WIFE.

Let him who would married be,
Look about him and take care
How he choose to take a wife—
    Take a wife,
Lest he rue it all his life !

If thou shoulds't make up thy mind,
And should take too young a wife,
Youthful wife has boiling blood—
    Boiling blood ;
No one thinks she is too good !

If thou shoulds't make up thy mind,
And shoulds't take too old a wife,
In the house she'll creep about—
    Creep about,
And will frighten people out !

If thou shoulds't make up thy mind,
And shoulds't take a handsome wife,
She will nought but trouble give—
    Trouble give ;
Others' visits she'll receive !

As for poor ones, let them be,
Nothing they will bring to thee,
Every thing will wanting be—
    Wanting be ;
Not a soul will come to thee !

If thou shoulds't make up thy mind,
And shoulds't take a wealthy wife,

Then with patience thou must bear—
   Thou must bear,
For the breeches she will wear!

Pretty, modest, smart, and neat,
Good and pious she must be;
If thou weddest such a wife—
   Such a wife,
Thou'lt not rue it all thy life!

But with all the devotion of the Slavonic races to the grand passion, it does not seem that the "course of true love" runs any smoother with them than it does with other people, as the following Servian song will show. It should be introduced, however, with the explanation already made—that in all the Slavonic nations the authority of the parents over their children in the affair of marriage is absolute; and the additional remark that their authority does not cease with marriage. It seems, indeed, that the parents, during their lives, exercise an important influence over the families of their children. The knowledge of this custom is necessary to the full understanding of the following little piece, entitled

THE QUARREL.

Come, my neighbors, let us hurry,
   That we may not stay out late;
My mother-in-law is in a fury—
   She says I broke my husband's pate.

Well, he would n't mind my wishes,
   Heeding not a word I said;
He refused to wash the dishes—
   I threw a pitcher at his head!

> Both were broken—head severely,
>   For the head I could but laugh ;
> But I loved my pitcher dearly—
>   It cost an apple and a half !

Those who are familiar with old English poetry
written before the age of Spenser, will notice many
resemblances between that and the poetry of the
Russians. Indeed—human nature being ever the
same—wherever nations have attained to a similar
degree of civilization and intelligence, they will be
found to resemble one another in their literature and
manners. And persons of the same degree of culture generally have similar opinions and tastes. The
upper castes of India, although we are in the habit of
thinking of that nation as sunk in idolatry, which
indeed is quite true as to the general masses, enter-
tain opinions on most matters of thought and taste
corresponding wth the educated classes of Germany,
France, or England, or indeed any other cultivated
nation. External manners may vary according to
local customs, and fashions may change, chameleon-
like, but modes of thought and matters of feeling
and taste, amongst the cultivated, have an affinity
throughout the world.

It is quite unsatisfactory to give extracts from prose
works without extending them impracticably. From
works of philosophy they would be unmeaning without the argument; from essays unfair, unless the
premises were stated ; and from stories scarcely intel-
ligible, unconnected with the plot; indeed, anything
torn from its context must necessarily suffer much
injury thereby. We must therefore be contented
with the following passages, taken from Turgenief's

" *Nest of Nobles*," which give certain marked characteristics of each sex :

" In her youth, Maria Demitrievna had enjoyed
the reputation of being a pretty blonde, and even in
her fiftieth year her features were not unattractive,
though they had lost somewhat of their fineness
and delicacy. She was naturally sensitive and im-
pressionable, rather than actually good-hearted, and
even in her years of maturity she continued to be-
have in the manner peculiar to ' institute girls.' She
denied herself no indulgence, she was easily put out
of temper, and she would even burst into tears if her
habits were interfered with. On the other hand, she
was gracious and affable when all her wishes were ful-
filled, and when nobody opposed her in anything.
Her house was the pleasantest in the town, and she
had a handsome income, the greater part of which was
derived from her late husband's earnings, and the
rest from her own property. Her two daughters
lived with her; her son was being educated in one of
the best crown establishments at St. Petersburgh.

" The old lady, who was sitting at the window with
Maria Demitrievna, was her father's sister, the aunt
with whom she had formerly spent so many lonely
years at Poknovskoe. Her name was Marfa Timofeevna Pestof. She was looked upon as an original,
being a woman of an independent character, who
bluntly told the truth to every one, and who, although her means were very small, behaved in society just as she would have done had she been rolling
in wealth. She never could abide the late Kalitine,
and as soon as her niece married him, she retired to
her own modest little property, where she spent ten

whole years in a peasant's smoky hut. Maria Demitrievna was rather afraid of her. Small in stature,
with black hair, a sharp nose, and eyes which even
in old age were still keen, Marfa Timofeevna walked
briskly, held herself bolt upright, and spoke quickly
but distinctly, and with a loud, high-pitched voice.
She always wore a white cap, and a white busk always formed a part of her dress." . . . .

" Panshine really was very adroit—not less so than
his father had been. And, besides this, he was en-
dowed with no small talent ; nothing was too difficult
for him. He sang pleasantly, could draw confidently,
and write poetry, and acted remarkably well.

" He was now only in his twenty-eighth year, but
he was already a chamberlain, and he had arrived at a
highly respectable rank in the service. He had thor-
ough confidence in himself, in his intellect, and in his
sagacity. He went onward under full sail, boldly
and cheerfully ; the stream of his life flowed smoothly
along. He was accustomed to please every one, old
and young alike ; and he imagined that he thoroughly understood his fellow creatures, especially
women—that he was intimately acquainted with all
their ordinary weaknesses.

"As one who was no stranger to art, he felt within
himself a certain enthusiasm, a glow, a rapture, in
consequence of which he claimed for himself various
exceptions from ordinary rules. He led a somewhat
irregular life ; he made acquaintances with people
who were not received into society, and in general he
behaved in an unconventional and unceremonious
manner. But in his heart of hearts he was cold and
astute ; and even in the midst of his most extrava-

gant rioting, his keen hazel eye watched and took note of everything. It was impossible for this daring and unconventional youth ever quite to forget himself, or to be thoroughly carried away. It should be mentioned to his credit, by the way, that he never boasted of his victories. To Maria Demitrievna's house he had obtained access, as soon as he arrived in O., and he soon made himself thoroughly at home in it. As to Maria Demitrievna herself, she thought there was nobody in the world to be compared with him." . . .

The current literature of Russia was checked and changed by the Crimean war; indeed, during that period, not a single book of the first class appeared, either in Germany, France, England or Russia. There were many books written at that time, but they nearly all relate in some way to the war, and of course are of an ephemeral character. The same may be said of that spawn of books produced by our late civil war. They are but little better than daily newspaper matter, and, having served their temporary purpose, are now quite worthless except as material for the future historian. It is impossible to write of current events with full information, if it, indeed, could be done with entire fairness. Even Thucydides did but little more than collect material for the Peloponnesian war, as much as his works are admired. Man is unable to rise above the events which press upon him, and view them entirely free from interest, prejudice, or passion, as he may look upon those which affected a preceding century or generation. The history of the present must be written in the future. Literature never flourishes when the world

is disturbed by wars; this fact is fully established by
the history of the past, but it generally receives an
impetus soon after war, or any great national disturb-
ance.   Ideas become shaken up during war, danger,
or any intense excitement, and, after the events are
past, fall into order again, and seek expression in
literature.   Nothing could have been more favorable
to awaken the genius of a people than the alternate
storm and calm of the Grecian States.   After the
Crimean war, which shook the entire Eastern hemisphere, and indeed disturbed the relations of the
whole world, a new vigor was infused into the literature of the nations, more especially of those so
deeply affected by that terrible conflict, so singularly
are the events of the world connected together in af-
fecting the destiny of man.   Within six years after
the peace of Paris, which settled the Crimean war,
schools were established in Russia which taught the
liberal and advanced philosophy of the time, and did
much to spread knowledge throughout the empire.
The works of Tyndall, Huxley, Darwin, Buckle,
Faraday, Mill, Helmholtz, Virchow, and of other liberal writers, were translated into the Russian language,
passed through several editions, and were circulated
widely.   Among the present novelists of Russia—
besides Turgenef, already noticed—may be mentioned
Avdeyef, Gontchasof, Krestovski, and Panayef;
among the present poets, Palouski and Nekrasof;
and dramatists, Ostrovski and Count Tolstoi.   Their
present great philosopher, and indeed it might be
said their first, is Lavrof; and their historians, Pypin,
Kovalevski, and Solovief.   Their great statesman,
during the Crimean and Austro-French wars was

Prince Gortschakof—the rival if not the equal of Bismarck., Daily and weekly newspapers, monthly and qarterly periodicals, have been established in several places in Russia, especially in St. Petersburgh and Moscow. Amongst their distinguished editors may be named Korsh, Krayefski, Katkof, and Aksakof. Besïdes these, there are many young authors rising in Russia in the various departments of literature, which, at this distance from them, seem rather as nebulæ than as fixed stars. It is not likely that this advancement of learning in. Russia—at least not for a long time—would have occurred, but for the stirring events connected with the Crimean war. Events affect men more than men affect events. Had there been no Trojan war, there never had been a Homer; had there been no civil-war in Rome, there never had been a Cæsar; had France, Spain, Italy, and Germany been at peace, there never had been a Charlemagne; had Russia, Poland, and Denmark treated Sweden fairly, there never had been a Charles the Twelfth ; if the nations of Europe had remained at peace, no Napoleon could have risen ; and but for our revolution Washington would probably have remained a private citizen. Indeed, it is impossible to be great in anything unless the circumstances necessary to greatness exist. When there is nothing to do, nothing can be done. The architect can not erect his edifice without material, nor can the sculptor produce his work without his marble. Men of genius affect one another; and they seem to grow in clusters. Aristotle, Socrates, and Plato flourished together; Cicero, Cæsar, and Sallust; Corneille, Moliere, and Racine ; Goethe, Schiller, and Herder ; Ad-

dison, Pope, and Johnson; the world has yet produced
but one Shakespeare. Russia has not yet offered her
cluster of geniuses, but if she continues to progress
in enlightenment as she has recently progressed, the
world may expect from her something far better than
anything she has yet produced. But she has already
afforded much that is good, some that is excellent,
though with some defects; yet it must be remembered that her literature is in a transition state. It
has not yet passed the first poetic condition; its
mass of polite prose literature is yet to be written,
after which a more profound, philosophic period may
be expected. It is a curious fact in the history of
literature that poetry precedes prose, and prose philosophy; but poetry also seems to be the last gift of
a nation to the world, as·well as the first, and many
believe the best. We have already remarked that
poetical expression precedes even civilization. The
poetical period begins before the language is per-
fected; as it becomes polished and full it passes into
prose; at length, after it has become settled, clear,
and certain, it is then suitable to express the various
philosophical formulæ and the exact sciences. We
do not mean to say that poetry and prose may not
exist together, and with philosophy and science; they
undoubtedly may, and do, after the philosophic period has arrived, and that of poetry, which is first
and last of all. In English literature, Addison,
Goldsmith, and Byron lived after Bacon, Locke, and
Newton; yet Gower, Chaucer, and Spenser preceded
all. Examples of this order of succession may be
cited from almost any nation. Not only Homer,
but also Sophocles and Æschylus preceded Herodo-

tus in Greece, and all of them lived before Socrates, Plato, and Aristotle. Ennius, Plautus, and Terence preceded Cicero, Pliny, and Sallust, and flourished before the philosophic period of Rome. Dante preceded Petrarch, and Petrarch ushered in Boccacio and other accomplished prose writers of Italy. Corneille, Moliere, and Racine introduced the period of prose composition in France; and Gower and Spenser flourished in England before any established prose writers, and prior to Bacon, Locke, and Newton. America is yet too young to afford an example of so grand a law; besides, when she became a distinct nation there was a literature in her language already formed. Indeed, America never can have an entirely new literature; her literature was begun for her before she had a beginning as a nation—before she was separated from the mother country. Yet there is enough room for originality in America, with her vast continent, free institutions, and new conditions; but whatever she may produce, English and American literature, being created by the same race, and expressed in the same language, must forever remain but separate parts of a grand whole. Russia, as we have seen, has produced her poets—some of distinction—and prose writers, not without merit. She has her philosophers, and may be said to be entering upon her scientific period. Her language is becoming more and more perfect as she progresses, and when war ceases to be her ruling passion she will take full rank in the peaceful pursuit of letters. What is to be the ultimate destiny of the Russian government, or of Russian literature, it is impossible to know, and, of course, idle to conjecture, but I can not help but think that she will carry her banner in the course of time to the Cape of Good Hope. The Slavi bear a relation to the nations south of their territory similar to that which the hardy North Men, in the earlier centuries of the Christian era, bore to the Roman Empire. They overran Rome and spread into the forests of Germany and Gaul, passed into France and England, and across to America. We derive our blood from their veins. They were a rude people, as rude as the Slavi ever were; yet out of this blood have sprung the best governments, the purest literature, and the politest nations of the earth. If the Slavonic race should run the same course they will but do what the Teutonic and Gallic have done. Russia must ultimately and inevitably be the great power of that hemisphere, as the United States must be of this. In her present position Russia has the finest opportunity to present a new literature to the world of any nation on earth. There never really has been a wholly new literature since the days of Greece; perhaps there never can be; but Russia is influenced less by the past than any other nation. Literature originally sprang up in the East, no one can tell exactly where or when. It ran through Assyria, Persia, Arabia, and all the eastern nations, into Egypt. Greece copied Egypt, Rome copied Greece, and the world has copied all. These two last mentioned and most celebrated nations have shot their influence in letters through Germany, France, Spain (less in Spain), England, and America, down to the present time. They must inevitably affect every portion of the world that comes in contact with their literature;

indeed, there remained a slavish obedience to classic models till Shakespeare, Cervantes, and a few other geniuses taught the world that it might be pleased without obeying the arbitrary rules of Greece and Rome—that we still have the common fountains of nature to draw from, and that, as these fountains are inexhaustible, we might still hope to taste of something fresh from their sources.

But whatever may be the fate of the Russian government, her learned belong to the Great Republic of Letters; and whatever may be the fate of all the political governments of the earth, the Republic of Letters will endure with the existence of the human mind. It has no limit in boundary save the earth itself. It began with the earliest history of man, and can end only with humanity. In commenced in the far East, and in the deep past, spread into Egypt, and continued on through Greece, Rome, Germany, France, Italy, Spain, England, Russia, to America; and although wars have continued, and still continue between the nations of the earth, and revolution has succeeded revolution within the separate governments, yet the Republic of Letters has marched onward in its peaceful career, binding together all the races of the world in one harmonious and indissoluble union. How temporary, and even trifling, appear the political revolutions of nations, when compared with the illustrious progress of letters. And it can have no retrograde movement; its march must ever be onward. The learned of all periods, and of all nations, and of all time, are members of this renowned Republic. Still may we go to the temple and sit at the banquet with Manu, Confucius,

Hafiz and Zoroaster of the East; with Soter and
Philadelphus, of Egypt; with Homer, Socrates,
Xenophon, Pindar, Plato, Aristotle, and Demos-
thenes, of Greece; with Virgil, Horace, Tacitus,
Seneca, Sallust, and Cicero, of Rome; with Goethe,
Schiller, Klopstock, Lessing, Herder, and Richter, of
Germany: with Corneille, Moliere, Racine, Voltaire,
Beranger, Lamartine, and Guizot, of France; with
Garcillasso, Herera, and Cervantes, of Spain; with
Dante, Petrarch, Boccacio, and Tasso, of Italy;
with Chaucer, Spenser, Shakespeare, Milton, Locke,
Newton, Addison, Johnson, Goldsmith, and Buckle,
of England; with Burns and Scott, of Scotland; with
Lomanosof, Karamzin, Pushkin, Dershavin, and
Zagorkin, of Russia; and with our own Franklin,
Bancroft, Bryant, Webster, and Irving, of America;
nor can we name a thousandth part of the worthy
guests, nor have we mentioned even all the nations;
while the feast is made richer and richer by the fruits
of mind through all the ages; more beautiful and
more beautiful with the sweetest blossoms of the
heart from every clime; and purer and purer by the
aspirations of the soul of all mankind. A seat at
this board offers a nobler ambition, and affords a
more rational honor than all the venal thrones and
high places of the earth; yea, to be the humblest
citizen in this world-wide and time-enduring Republic, is a prouder title than all that kings, and crowns,
and the powers of the earth can bestow.